TOP SIDE HUSTLE FROM HOME 2020:

7 Simple, Proven Ideas to Start Your Successful Lifestyle Business From Home Today

LEGAL

© Copyright (2020) by V. K. PAYSON - All rights reserved worldwide.

This document is geared towards providing exact and reliable information in regards to the topic and issue covered. The publication is sold with the idea that the publisher is not required to render accounting, officially permitted, or otherwise, qualified services. If advice is necessary, legal or professional, a practiced individual in the profession should be ordered.

- From a Declaration of Principles which was accepted and approved equally by a Committee of the American Bar Association and a Committee of Publishers and Associations.

In no way is it legal to reproduce, duplicate, or transmit any part of this document in either electronic means or in printed format. Recording of this publication is strictly prohibited and any storage of this document is not allowed unless with written permission from the publisher. All rights reserved.

The information provided herein is stated to be truthful and consistent, in that any liability, in terms of inattention or otherwise, by any usage or abuse of any policies, processes, or directions contained within is the solitary and utter responsibility of the recipient reader. Under no circumstances will any legal responsibility or blame be held against the publisher for any reparation, damages, or monetary loss due to the information herein, either directly or indirectly. Respective authors own all copyrights not held by the publisher.

The information herein is offered for informational purposes solely, and is universal as so. The presentation of the information is without contract or any type of guarantee assurance.

The trademarks that are used are without any consent, and the publication of the trademark is without permission or backing by the trademark owner. All trademarks and brands within this book are for clarifying purposes only and are the owned by the owners themselves, not affiliated with this document.

CONTENTS

Introduction

Secret 1: YouTube: The Golden Goose

Secret 2: Affiliate Marketing: The Easy Way

Secret 3: Alibaba -- Wholesale Magic

Secret 4: Merch by Amazon: A Hidden Gem

Secret 5: Shopify: Sell Your Own Products

Secret 6: Money is Just a Smartphone Away

Secret 7: The Freelancer Way

Conclusion

INTRODUCTION

Mindset

Hello, and thank you for downloading this book. If you're reading this, then you must have a question -- shared by millions around the world -- that needs answering: how can I make more money? In this book, you can expect to find answers to that question.

We will take you on a journey to unravel the secrets of having a successful side hustle. In this quick and effortless read, you will learn how you can start earning money alongside your day job, and you won't have to wait for years until you reap the rewards of your efforts.

Countless people are suffering through financially challenging times in 2020, with the COVID-19 pandemic and layoffs affecting millions worldwide. If you can relate to this, then we urge you to use this ordeal as motivation. With the resources and ideas outlined in this book you can pick yourself up and come back stronger than ever. Your future self will most certainly thank you for it.

We have created a guide with beginner-friendly instructions to help anyone start making an additional income in 30 days or less.

With others, you will need to work every time you need to earn, and the rewards are quite lucrative. The great thing about the financial precepts outlined in this book is that you don't need massive initial capital; this is a near-zero upfront investment kind of deal for most opportunities mentioned.

You will learn about surprisingly secrets and tips that can help you find the best side-hustle from home or evenget closer to that dream of financial independence and freedom. You're building your own money machine, not anyone else's. These are not scams or unrealistic promises; they're genuine recipes for success. If you follow it and believe in yourself, the sky truly is the limit.

Now that you know what awaits you in this book, take a deep breath, and let's get started.

SECRET 1:

YouTube-The Golden Goose

In case you were unaware, YouTube is one of the best ways you can generate passive income online. With its significant reach, YouTube has allowed content creators to earn passive income by monetizing their skills, talents, and expertise in various domains.

However, making money off YouTube isn't as straightforward as most people think. It's more than just 'create a video, upload it, and make money off each view from ads'. Statistics show that you can make around $1,000 per half a million views, which isn't lucrative unless you generate a billion views per video.

In other words, you cannot earn solid passive income based on the YouTube ad revenue stream alone, because most of the money that advertisers pay to promote their products doesn't directly go to the content creators (you).

So, how can you make a worthwhile passive income off YouTube? Diversify. You cannot rely solely on the revenue stream from ads, as we mentioned, so you'll have to explore other sources to make that dream income.

That said, this doesn't mean you should miss out on the ad revenue altogether. Here's how to start generating money from creating content on YouTube.

1) Create an AdSense Account

Ultimately, you are a content creator, and you want to make money from your views and monetize that content. To do that, the first step you need to take is to create an AdSense account. This step comes right after signing up for a YouTube account -- which most people already have anyway since it's linked to your Google account.

After setting up your YouTube account, you need to create an account Adsense, which is how you run ads on your videos. AdSense is the main advertising engine used by Google sites and its partner websites. You will be asked to provide details like personal payment information, social security number, and other tax-related information when you create an AdSense account.

2) Finding Niche Content

So far, we've mentioned basic information that you can easily figure out, but this is where things get interesting. With a YouTube and AdSense account, you are ready to start monetizing your content; but what kind of content are you going to be creating?

As we mentioned earlier, views don't get you that much money from ads. Nevertheless, you can increase the amount you get per view by creating niche content where advertisers often pay more. Here is when you really need to pause for a second and figure things out.

The niche you will invest your time and energy in will reflect how your channel stands out, and you can't easily shift niches after a year or two because you'd lose subscribers and views.

What you need to do at this stage is to find profitable niches that can earn you more money than standard content where advertisers pay a minimum amount per view. To do this, research YouTube competitive keywords using platforms like KeywordTool.io to find those keywords with the highest cost per click (CPC).

In fields like real estate and insurance, you will find that advertisers pay considerably more money so that they can reach consumers and grab their attention. In contrast, you have fields like cooking and food recipes with a much lower CPC. So, use keyword tools in the niche you're considering to optimize your content best and make real money off ads.

3) Creating Content

If anyone assures you that there is a blueprint for creating viral content on YouTube, they'd be lying. Some of the most viewed videos on the platform are families doing family things, recorded with a cheap phone camera. Yet, you will also find professionally shot and produced music videos with billions of views.

At this point, you already know the niche you'll be creating content in. What comes next is deciding how you will be creating that content. Will you use your smartphone camera and microphone, or will you invest in high-quality equipment? Which works best with the kind of content you are planning to create?

Ask yourself these questions and get the necessary gear for your videos, even if it's just a phone or a cheap condenser microphone. You need to practice using video editing tools like the free Windows Movie Maker or Adobe Premiere if you want more features. Remember to avoid using copyrighted images and music on your videos, or else YouTube can take your content down for infringement violation.

4) Alternative Means to Generate Money

By now, you will have created content and started making little revenue off ads on your videos, which still won't be enough. So, how can you start making those large sums to earn a comfortable passive income? Fortunately, there are several things you can do.

Sponsorships: The first way you can earn money off the videos you create is by attracting sponsorships. The great thing about this option is that you don't have to pay YouTube a cut of your earnings. These deals are usually sought out by the content creators themselves, or sponsors reaching out if the channel has a large following.

There is a trend that you can easily observe with the most successful YouTubers; they have sponsorships and advertisements in their video recordings, and they promote certain products that fit into the context of their channels. You can leverage this too.

Also, you'll get to negotiate with the advertiser on whether you want your contract to be based on views, impressions, or the general size of your audience. This way, you'll be making money conveniently off sponsorships as well as YouTube ads.

Affiliate Links: In this upcoming chapter, we will discuss affiliate marketing and how you can use it to generate a significant passive income, but for now, we're talking about YouTube specifically.

Using affiliate links can help generate significant revenues for any content creator on this platform. You can create content around a certain product -- a phone, camera, mobile case, etc. -- and then add a link in the video description to inform your viewers where to buy said products.

Whenever one of them clicks on the link and buys the product, you get a commission agreed upon earlier with the seller. The bigger your channel grows, the more people buy through your affiliate links and the more money you make.

Sell Your Own Products: Another tactic used by video creators on YouTube is to create their own products and services and sell them through their YouTube channels and videos. YouTube is the second-largest search engine globally after Google, so it is the ideal platform to promote products of your own making.

Whether it is digital services or physical goods like t-shirts and custom mugs, you stand to make a lot of money selling those products. People look up your videos, like your product, and they open the attached links and buy them. Most importantly, they are your own products, so no one gets a cut out of the revenues.

This is how you can create videos on YouTube and monetize them for a steady, passive income. Many people work full-time on their YouTube channels, and some make millions out of the ads, sponsorships, and other approaches we mentioned earlier. You can get there too!

Remember that the most important thing is to deliver engaging, valuable content that will cater to your target audience. Do that, and there is no limit to the number of views you can get and the many benefits you'd earn with them.

SECRET 2:
Affiliate Marketing: The Easy Way

Affiliate marketing is one of the best and most accessible techniques for making a passive income, and just about anyone can do it. Like YouTube, some make up to $3,000 a day; others get a revenue of well over $10,000! So, there's definitely money in it if you know what you're doing. Here's how you can get started.

What Is Affiliate Marketing?

It's quite simple. As an affiliate marketer, you find a product or a service that you like and wish to promote. You then search for affiliate programs online that can help you do that, sign up for the program in question, after which you will get an affiliate link that is specific to you.

Next, you start creating content about the product

or service that you like and insert that affiliate link throughout your content. Whenever a user clicks the link and makes a purchase, you will get a commission -- a percentage of the product or service's sale.

Essentially, you're promoting a seller's service or product, and you get paid each time someone uses your affiliate link to conduct a purchase.

The great thing about affiliate marketing is how cheap and accessible it is. You don't need fancy cameras and microphones, much less a studio setup (although it does help if you're on YouTube). All you need is a domain for your website, which costs around $9 a year. For more information about building website, check out mailcheimp.com.

Once you're all set, you can sign up for affiliate programs free of charge and start creating content using those affiliate links. Remember that you're not creating a product or a service, so that's definitely less time and energy-consuming; you merely promote other people's products without having to worry about the process that goes behind creating those products (research, conception, testing, etc.).

Now, how can you start earning money through affiliate marketing?

1. Find a Niche

Before you can start earning money, you need to find a niche to create content and earn commissions. It can't just be any random niche. It must be something you know, are good at, or are passionate about -- ideally, all three.

This is the most important step throughout your affiliate marketing journey, and you need to give it some serious thought because everything hinges on the niche you choose. Of course, there are more competitive and lucrative markets out there that you can opt for, but who is to say that this is the best option for you?

If you can't create engaging content in your niche, people simply won't visit your blog or website. If they don't do that, you don't get paid. As such, you need to select something that you can generate quality content around regularly.

Having prior knowledge about the niche is certainly helpful, but you need to have hands-on experience to create compelling content. For instance, you can't create a blog about smartphone reviews and not test or use the devices you talk about.

If your specialty is digital marketing services, you need a solid understanding of web design, WordPress, and SEO. These are examples of how you should be involved in your niche because this will be your bread and butter.

So, don't go and choose a field you know nothing about and believe you can generate content through research; it might work for your few first tries, but it's not a viable strategy in the long run.

2. Create the Platform

To create content around a product or a service, first and foremost, you need a platform. The best way to go here is a blog, and it is the strategy used by many of the world's most successful affiliate marketers.

You can have a dedicated YouTube channel, but this is the less commonly used approach by affiliate marketers -- it is still very effective, and a successful YouTube channel will get you plenty of affiliate link clicks. But for this section, let's focus on blogs since those are easier to set up and handle.

The best way to create your website's design is by using WordPress, which can help you build a professional and good-looking blog quickly and efficiently. As we mentioned earlier, purchasing a domain costs little to nothing, and it's the main investment you need to make for this business endeavor.

One of the best things about creating blogs is how simple and easy it is; virtually anyone can do it. Just take your time in creating the blog or website, and don't undermine any detail.

The quality of the navigation and the layout of the website play a crucial role in your search engine ranking, which is very important, as we'll explain later on.

3. Find an Affiliate Program

Now that you know your niche and have selected the platform on which you'll create your content, it is time to start looking for an affiliate program so you can start earning. This step is easy since most products and services sold online have associated affiliate programs that you can partner with.

You can start looking at websites of products and services that you already use; they often have tabs on the top or the bottom of the page for affiliate programs, and you can sign up with any of these without trouble.

You may also want to consider joining an affiliate network, which are businesses that connect sellers and service providers with affiliate marketers so that both can strike a deal and earn real money.

There are many advantages to joining such networks, and they give you plenty of helpful features and data to help you make a better product selection and earn higher profits from your affiliate links. There are plenty of networks out there like Amazon associates, ClickBank, and CJ Affiliate.

One last approach you can use to find affiliate programs is simply typing the product or service name that you want to promote plus 'affiliate programs,' and you'll get search results with the programs you can join.

4. Creating Content

Now that everything is set, you are ready to create your content. Having a great looking blog and enrolling in a ton of affiliate programs won't serve any purpose if you don't create engaging content so that users can find your blog and purchase via your affiliate links. Since we're focusing on blogs here, there are a few points to bear in mind.

You can't create content and force your affiliate links inside the articles and hope people will click them; they must fit into the context of the post naturally for users to even consider clicking and making the purchase.

Most importantly, when it comes to affiliate marketing, it is all about the value and quality of your products. Anyone can create blog posts around any of the millions of products and services online, but does that mean people will automatically click on your blog and then your links?

Not necessarily. Your content has to be interesting and of high-quality. It needs to present readers with something that they don't already know, answers their questions, or keep them entertained. If you create content that checks these boxes, then you will have struck gold.

5. SEO

If you want people to find your blog, know that

investing in search engine optimization is not a luxury. Many novices create random content and insert affiliate links throughout, hoping for the best. This strategy won't do you much good, and it won't achieve your passive income goals.

As we mentioned earlier, you need to create high-quality content, and SEO is one of the basics of doing so. With a niche in mind, you have a target audience that you want to reach -- the people who are most likely to interact with your posts and click on your affiliate links.

SEO is how online users find your blog on search engines. The more optimized your content is, the higher it will rank on search results, and the more easily people will find it.

The first thing you need to do to optimize your content is to add keywords. Depending on the topic you'll be covering in your content, there needs to be keywords throughout the article -- placed naturally -- that will lead people right to your posts.

Those posts should contain the strategically placed affiliate links, which need to be placed early on in the article, and, again, they need to fit into the article in a way that doesn't scream promotional.

Note: If you're going to add many affiliate links on your blog, remember to add an affiliate link plugin. This is a very important tool for affiliate marketers. After a few months or even years of doing this, you will have hundreds of affiliate links throughout your blog.

Some of those might need updating or even replacing after they have expired. Without the plugin, you'll spend countless hours searching for those links manually, which is time-consuming and will be a missed opportunity if someone clicks on an expired link. With a plugin, you can sort and manage those links easily.

Tips

Personalize: Keeping your content personalized and specific is of the essence. This is how your content can resonate with readers and, hopefully, translate into sales and future revenues. Your content needs to be relevant, and you should speak from experience about the product or service you're promoting.

Make the reader feels like you know what you're talking about, and you're not just some marketer promoting a product just to get a commission.

Mix things up: While your blog or website is based around a certain niche, that doesn't mean you should not diversify your content and mix things up. This will help you keep readers interested and hooked to your content since you're continuously giving them something new and interesting.

Instead of only writing product reviews, try creating a tutorial. Send emails or newsletters, and change your format now and then to keep people intrigued.

Invest in Quality: If you can't commit to creating quality content regularly, it might be a good idea to hire someone who can. As mentioned earlier, this is your main source of income, and if there is a drop in quality, people won't engage with what you have to offer.

As such, you will lose both recognition and money. Content aside, don't try to save money on web hosting, stay away from free themes; invest in making your blog presentable and attractive. These are SEO factors that make a huge difference in your search engine ranking and, consequently, your conversion rate.

SECRET 3:

Alibaba — Wholesale Magic

Up next in our list of side hustle secrets for young people is Alibaba. How can you make money off the Chinese giant? The strategy that many have used successfully is importing products from Alibaba and selling them on platforms like Amazon, and it works like a charm! Here's what you need to do.

Finding the Right Product

If you are serious about this business endeavor, pay attention to this first step as it is the most important. For starters, you need to generate successful product ideas.

What kind of products do you want to sell? This question will require a good deal of research. Start by asking people what they want. People always have needs that need to be fulfilled and the products that they want to buy. So, using platforms like

Reddit and Facebook, ask which products people think are in a shortage.

You should also start with yourself; are there certain products you constantly have a hard time finding? If there are, what is the reason behind that?

New product ideas aside, conduct a little research on Amazon and other e-commerce platforms to find out what their best-selling products are, not so you can import and sell them, but to get inspiration.

Perhaps you can adjust the product somehow and then sell it in a different light, which is a successful strategy that can potentially make waves in the market. You can't just buy from Alibaba the same products that competitors are selling on Amazon; this won't earn you any money.

You need unique products that will solve a problem or fill a need for the average user. That way, you can order those products from Alibaba and sell them wherever you are, and however you please.

What Items to Import

As established, your product needs to solve a problem, but it also needs to have certain specifications.

You need lightweight, practical products. When you get a lightweight product that you know (from previous research) people want or need, you can get it at an affordable price and sell it yourself at a competitive and reasonable price.

When the product is lightweight, it is easier to return it to China if there is any reason to do so. Purchasing heavy items from China and then returning them can be a very complicated process. Needless to say, lightweight items also cost you less in shipping and handling.

The product should also be simple and sober in its design. The last thing you need is a complicated electronic device that will be worthless if it presents the tiniest defect.

In a nutshell, look for simple and lightweight items located in a price range between $20 and $200, which is ideal for middle-class shoppers looking for a bargain.

Is It Safe to Shop from Alibaba?

If you plan on purchasing items in bulk from Alibaba to sell them, this question will have certainly crossed your mind. The answer is, it can be.

There are scammers on Alibaba, but the platform also hosts some of the best Chinese manufacturers. The key is knowing to distinguish between the two, finding the reliable one, and dealing with those.

There are plenty of options on Alibaba, but your best bet will be dealing exclusively with Gold Suppliers, the website's premium sellers. Those are the ones that pay the website to appear higher in search results, and they are credible and legitimate.

Start Slow

In general, it's always a good idea to get Alibaba's trade assurance program, which protects your orders and reduces the risk of getting scammed by a supplier, with money-back guarantees in some cases. Even with such protection, you should still take it slowly and not rush into buying products in bulk from China.

You need to get a few samples of the product first to see if it works as it should and inspect its quality. If it checks out, conduct test runs, and try to sell it on Amazon, or however, you plan on selling it. Note how fast it sells and seek feedback from your clients.

This kind of pragmatism and meticulousness is how you can stay in business and grow this passive income strategy. Buying in bulk without thorough prior considerations is the easiest way to waste your money.

It might be tricky to get lower minimum order quantity from wholesale merchants, but you need to be subtle and convince them that you are in it for the long run. Explain that you first need to sample a few products because this is company policy or your boss' explicit request.

Tips

Shipping is complicated, so don't try to wrap your head around it. Just reach out to shipping companies and get an estimate of the costs so you can do the math and allocate funds accordingly.

One thing you should remember about shipping is that prices often vary with dates, much like airline tickets. So, play around with them until you get the best rate.

As far as product packaging, some people will ask the seller from Alibaba to ensure the product is properly packaged so you can sell it directly on Amazon without wasting more time and money.

In due time, you will be ordering in bulk from Alibaba, so it's important to have an inspection process. There are specialized companies that can inspect the product and the packaging for you, so ask around and dig a little to find one you can go in business with.

After doing all this, your products will be ready to go up on Amazon. Set up your account, add your products, and use sponsored ads to reach as many customers as possible. You should also use social media platforms like Facebook and Instagram to promote your products; they can help you generate many fresh leads.

SECRET 4:

Merch by Amazon:
A Hidden Gem

Merch by Amazon is one of the best ways to earn passive income, and it is also one of the least known approaches despite its enormous potential. Essentially, Merch by Amazon helps you create and sell branded products that are designed by you; only they are produced, sold, and shipped by Amazon.

This exempts you from any major associated costs. Merch is mostly used for t-shirt designs, and as Amazon puts it, they create the product page and handle all parts of the process for you with no upfront fees. In other words, Merch by Amazon is a print-on-demand service.

Getting Started

To join Merch by Amazon, simply head to the official landing page and log in with your Amazon ID.

You fill out a form with your personal information, and after that, wait for the formal acceptance email into Merch by Amazon's program.

The approval can take anything between three weeks and three months, so keep regularly checking until you receive confirmation. In the meantime, you need to get busy working on your designs.

Designing

Getting accepted into Merch is just the start. Next comes the real bulk of the work, where you get to design and sell your art. The first thing to keep in mind is you need more than just one design.

The more of them you have, the better your chances will be of making money. When you're first starting out with Merch, you can only have 25 designs, but that is only for a limited time. After selling your first 25 t-shirts, you get upgraded to a higher tier, where you can display up to 100 designs. After selling another 25, you'll get upgraded to a higher tier with more design options, and so forth.

Creating Your First T-Shirt

The process is fairly simple. You need to log into

your Merch dashboard, where you upload your designs and analyze your sales. Amazon also offers a template tool to help you size your PNG file placement on the shirt.

You can use Photoshop or whichever design software you're comfortable with, and after that, it's a walk in the park. Place the PNG file on the front and/or back of the t-shirt, depending on your design. Then, optimize the color and type of shirt and set the price. Finally, add a brand name and Amazon title for your t-shirt, and don't forget to write a compelling description for the product.

Market Your Shirts

Since you want people to find and purchase your t-shirts, you need to market them accordingly. Use whatever means at your disposal. Amazon has made it easy for you to create the t-shirts with your creative designs, but you need to put in a little extra effort to sell your designs.

Use various social media platforms (Facebook, Twitter, Instagram, Snapchat, etc.) to promote your products, and have your friends share your designs.

Tips

Keywords play a very important role in your sales success. Ensure your product descriptions are comprehensive, clear, and loaded with keywords that can lead many of the millions of Amazon users to your designs. You can do a little research beforehand and use keyword tools to learn about the relevant keywords for Merch by Amazon.

Always avoid copyright infringement so you don't have your designs taken down or your account suspended. If the design isn't all yours, don't put it up on Merch. Speaking of designs, find a niche market with unique and plentiful design ideas to have options.

If people get hooked on your brand of t-shirts, you can make a lot of money through Merch. Never use profanity or portray human tragedies, create designs that exploit children or minorities, or incorporate pornographic or sensitive materials.

Amazon takes a standard 15% as a listing fee. Also, you should know that t-shirts with printing on the back and front cost more to produce, so the price of making a double-sided t-shirt will be higher.

SECRET 5:

Shopify: Sell Your Own Products

With Alibaba, you import products from China to sell them at Amazon or elsewhere. Now, with Shopify, you get to sell your own products. Shopify is an all-inclusive e-commerce platform where people can promote, sell, and ship products while paying one monthly rate.

The great thing about Shopify is its low setup cost. It also comes with an intuitive interface that is easy to use and navigate. In short, Shopify is a superb option to start earning a secondary income in 2020, and it's a great side-hustle next to your day job.

The main benefit of using Shopify is that you have a lot of options. You don't necessarily have to sell products you design or create, but you obviously can if you want. There are different ways through which you can make money through this platform.

1. Drop-Shipping

What's great about this approach is how you don't need a warehouse or a full inventory to get into the business. You simply need to find a supplier willing to provide you with existing products; they will take care of packaging and fulfillment.

Then, you get to sell those products on Shopify. You don't need a large amount of money to start, and you also get to control the size of the shipments you're dealing in, which means you can start small and scale in time.

2. Thrift Store Purchases

Another great way to use Shopify is by selling the finds you come across in thrift shops. It is the perfect opportunity to turn a hobby or passion of yours into a lucrative business opportunity.

There are many interesting and unique items to be found in a thrift store, from collector's items to vintage t-shirts and paintings. If you can source such products and offer them for sale on Shopify, you can expect to make a good secondary income.

People are always looking for vintage and unique

items that won't cost a fortune, and if you manage to provide them with that, you've hit the jackpot.

3. Sell Your Own Products

Shopify is ideal for people who have a talent for crafting things and wish to monetize that talent. Are you good at making clothes? Why not start your own clothing line?

Shopify makes it easy for users to start fashion businesses, and they can connect you to apparel printers and clothing manufacturers. So, all you need is a design. This means you can start a clothing brand in a matter of days.

You can also sell your art online, and Shopify will give you a massive reach and promote your work to a wide audience. Whatever it is you want to sell, chances are Shopify can help you do it successfully.

4. Courses

If you have a concept for an online course, Shopify might just be everything you've dreamed of. You can create your online course and sell it through the platform for a significant passive income; every time someone purchases your online course, you make money. It's as simple as that.

This is ideal for people who have expertise, knowledge, or an in-demand skill that they want to share with others while earning money in the process.

How to Start:

1. Create an Account

The first step to earn money through Shopify is to create an account on the platform. The great thing about Shopify is it gives you a two-week free trial, which you can use to set up your online store and start adding products.

2. Store/Business Name and Logo

Since you'll be selling your products and services through Shopify, you need to next add your store or business name because this is the name through which people will find your products. This name will be associated with your domain, so you need to take your time selecting this one. You then need to come up with a logo for your brand.

3. Add Products

As we explained earlier, there are different ways for you to add your products. You need to either use drop shipping or create your own products, and in this step, you will add your products or services into the account and then start to set pricing.

4. Add Relevant Details

While setting up your store, you will be asked to add any relevant details, starting with shipping. You will select the type of your product (physical, for instance, if you're selling canned sauce), and then add its weight. The platform will then automatically calculate shipping rates from your storage to the clients.

5. SEO

Always remember to optimize your product page in every possible way so people could find your products. You want people to find your Shopify page every time they type 'canned sauce.' This means adding the necessary keywords, adding the correct page title, writing a thorough description of the products, and creating a unique but simple URL. All those details help you rank higher on search engine results, and in turn your products would reach more people.

SECRET 6:

Money is Just a Smartphone Away

This one is for the photographers out there, or those aspiring to become one. Brands and companies are always looking for stock videos and images to market their products and services. If you establish yourself in this market as someone who provides high-quality images and videos, you stand to make a lot of money.

The great thing about this side hustle is how it can cost you absolutely nothing to begin. Many of the images and videos that brands are looking for can be shot with a smartphone –– with newer models providing high specs that allow the capture of 4K and even 8K resolution videos with the latest flagships.

So, where do you start?

Find a Platform

There are plenty of platforms ready to purchase your stock content, and you should look for the one that best suits your needs. Platforms like Getty Images, Shutterstock, Pond5, Vimeo, and VideoHive, all provide similar services. That said, you should know that some platforms provide better rates than others.

For instance, with Shutterstock, you'll get 30 percent of the purchase price, which is set by the platform. On Pond5, however, you set the price and earn 50 percent on all sales. Does that mean one option is better than the other? Not necessarily; each platform has its pros and cons, and you need to weigh them against each other and select the best option for you.

How It Works

You start by uploading your footage to one of those platforms, set or agree on a price, and then wait for people to buy it. Customers purchase a license to use your content however they please. This is known as a royalty-free license, which means you still own the footage and can use it in any way that you want. You make money whenever someone purchases the license, and there is no limit on the number of licenses you can sell.

Read the Fine Print

The question you're probably considering right now is whether you can sell your stock footage on more than one platform. Generally speaking, you can. It will, however, depend on the contract you have with each platform.

This is why you need to read the fine print to check any restrictions over sharing your footage across multiple platforms.

Getty, for example, offers more money if you sell the footage exclusively on their platform. However, if you use more than one platform, you can make even more money. So, it's up to you to decide which path will be the most lucrative.

What Kind of Footage Should I Submit?

Aside from the footage being taken by you, the higher the quality of your videos and images, the better. Sure, vintage photos with a Polaroid or analog camera still hold their appeal, but that is a very niche market, and you'd be better off with high-resolution digital images.

Some categories of photography also work better than others. If you check the top categories on stock footage platforms, you will find that travel, animals, lifestyle, food, and sports are among the most in-demand stock footage.

SECRET 7:

The Freelancer Way

Last in our secrets to making a secondary income is online freelancing. If you possess a set of skills or experience in a particular field, you can monetize it and make money from the comfort of your home. The following points should help you get started.

Find a Niche

For starters, you need to determine the skill you're going to be using to make money. Fortunately, it does not have to be related to your day job; it can be something you're just good at or passionate about.

You may work by day as a banker, but you have always had excellent writing skills. So, why not make money off your writing? Perhaps you're a sales agent by day, but have a passion for video editing; you can make money off that passion by night. That doesn't mean you have to make a complete shift, though.

The easiest way to become a freelancer is to sell the experience you already have and secure extra gigs alongside your main occupation. Whatever it is, you need to find that skill you're going to monetize, and you need to work on perfecting it.

Understand the Market

It helps if you have a solid understanding of the market and what jobs are in demand on a freelance basis. Some jobs are in higher demand, and if there is an opportunity for you to develop a certain skill that you already possess to perform such jobs, then, by all means, take it. You'll find that some of the most needed freelancers are in the fields of editing, writing, proofing, translating, and web design.

If you have a foundation on which you can build to work in those fields, take some time to work on your skills so you can get there and start earning.

The Platforms

Thankfully, the internet is very generous when it comes to providing freelancers with the platforms they need to find jobs. With websites like Upwork, Freelancer, Fiverr, and much more, you can reach a large pool of clients and punctual missions.

You simply need to create a profile on those platforms, list your skills and experience, and then start applying for jobs or offering your services for clients to find you.

For some of these platforms, you will be asked to set your standard or hourly rates. For others, the client will have a fixed budget for the project, and you'll decide whether it suits your skills and experience.

What You Need

Other than a skill to sell, you will need a stable internet connection because most of your work will be conducted online. You will also need a laptop or a computer to work on, since most of your work will be done from home or wherever you want. It is a good idea to create a website for yourself to share it with potential clients. It makes you look reliable and professional, and it's your online storefront.

Steps to Start

1. Create account on freelancing platform

As explained earlier, after finding the specialty that you want to work in, you need to create an account on one of those platforms, say Upwork, for example. In this particular platform, you can take tests to prove your competence in certain fields, which are added to your profiles as badges to show potential clients that you're good. So, if you can take any such tests, do it.

2. Set Your Rates

One of the most important and difficult steps while starting out as a freelancer is setting your rates. You need to do a little research to learn about the average rates in your field, and set your rates as someone starting out accordingly.

You want to set competitive rates so you could compete with other freelancers who have more experience, but you don't want to set very low prices because it is bad for the market and it is also untrustworthy from a client's perspective. In short, find the average rates for that field and set your rates around that.

3. Bid for Jobs

In a platform like Upwork, you need to keep bidding for jobs so you can land your first client. This part is usually the hardest and it does take some time.

Don't lose patience, and keep applying until you get a client.

4. Maintain Quality

As a freelancer, your biggest asset is quality. When you do land that first client, you need to do a great job because this is how you make a name for yourself. If you maintain a high level of quality, clients will flock. If your quality ever dips, you will get bad reviews on freelancing platforms, and you will have a hard time finding clients.

5. Invest in Marketing

We mentioned earlier the importance of having your own website as a freelancer, and you need to invest in creating a great one. Don't skimp out on quality with this one. Make sure the navigation is smooth and the text is clear and spellchecked. Everything needs to be in order since this website will be used to promote your work on social media platforms as well as search engine results.

BONUS:

Save your time and money
You don't want to miss this.

TIMOTHY FERRISS is a serial entrepreneur, #1 New York Times bestselling author, and angel investor (Facebook, Twitter, Evernote, Uber, and 20+ more). Tim's book -- "The 4-Hour Workweek", has been published in 30+ languages, it has spent seven years on The New York Times bestseller list.

This book breaks the traditional concept of the work mode, I would recommend this book to anyone with aspirations to have more freedom in their life.

As a special bonus for my readers, I created this 1-page PDF, it's free! you can quickly get the core messages of this book, you don't have to spend 12.69$ and 10 hours! Just click the link here www.vkpayson.com/bonus, this PDF will be sitting in your inbox immediately.

IMPORTANT

If you've made it this far, you are probably a bit overwhelmed by the bulk of new information thrown at you. Sit back and take a moment to process it all.

Congratulations are in order; you're now ready to start your own side hustle. As you have learned by now, these are all legitimate online opportunities that can help you make a lot of money if you follow the tips outlined in this book. We hope we have managed to fill in the blanks and explain how this all works.

Success is never guaranteed in life, but with this book, you have a blueprint on how to achieve it. The next step is to get off the couch and put in the work needed to start earning! While these business opportunities may have looked easy in theory, they require a good deal of effort and tenacity to succeed, especially in the beginning.

Our recommendation is to read this again slowly and isolate the best opportunity for your skills and abilities. Don't try starting three or four different businesses all at once, no matter how tempting it may seem. Chances are, you will fail and lose money in the process. Each of these will require your full dedication and focus, and there is a learning curve to go through.

So, choose one of these secrets and start working through it until you get there. Don't stop until you start seeing results and getting the significant income that you're aiming for. It might take a couple of weeks to achieve, but the rewards are certainly worth it. Financial freedom might be a dream, but it is an attainable one. Always remember that.

If you enjoyed this guide and got helpful pointers and clear strategies from it, would you consider leaving a review? I'v made it as easy as possible for you, just click the link here. I want to let you know that your review is very important and will help me in ensuring that I improve this book and provide more value to your life. Thanks for your time and support!

www.ingramcontent.com/pod-product-compliance
Lightning Source LLC
Chambersburg PA
CBHW031550210526
45464CB00003B/1236